# A Child to Change Your Life

# A Child to Change Your Life

by Thomas D. Murray

GROSSET & DUNLAP
A FILMWAYS COMPANY
Publishers • New York

Designed by Al Schroeder

*All photographs by the author unless otherwise credited*

Copyright © 1976 by Thomas D. Murray
All rights reserved
Published simultaneously in Canada
Library of Congress catalog card number: 77-82001
ISBN 0-448-14380-1
First Grosset & Dunlap edition 1977
Printed in the United States of America

To Cindy and Susan.
To David and Piper.
And to Carol.

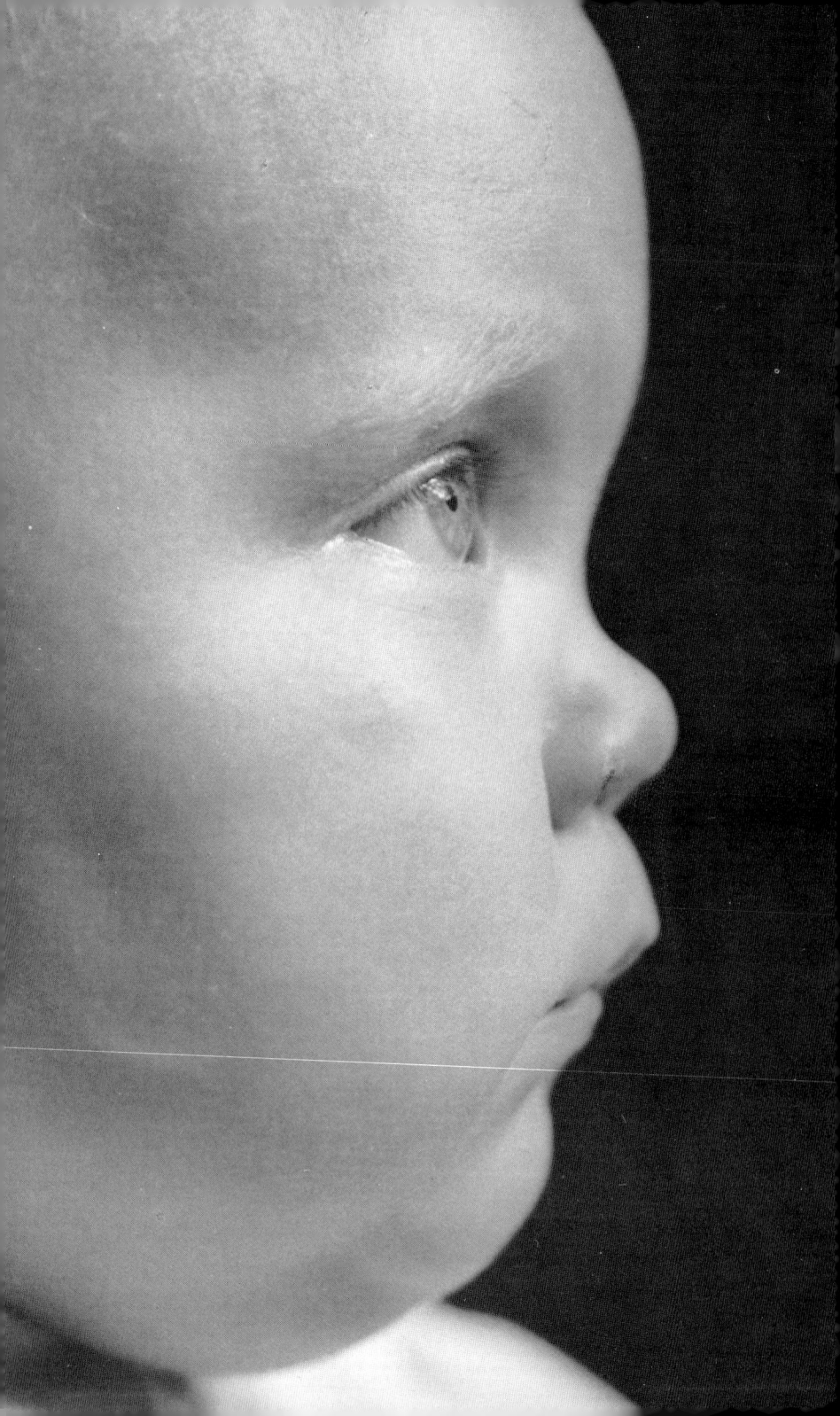

"Wait 'til you have children; your life will never be the same" has always sounded to me like a bit of pomposity — a kind of know-it-all expression on the part of some parent anxious to prove a veteran status on the subject of mother or fatherhood.

I always assumed the meaning behind those words to be nothing more than a magnificent grasp of the obvious, a warning of the predictable price of time and care and attention one must pay for pink, paper-thin ears, for button noses, for high white shoes and soft, round bottoms, for the utter pricelessness and loveliness of little people.

I know now I missed the point. Partly because most people aren't able to explain or go beyond the simple pronouncement that "a child will change your life". And partly because I was looking for the answer before it was looking for me.

I know now that what they're saying has nothing to do with the problems of finding baby-sitters or the privacy to make love — nothing to do with terrible colicky nights that are much too long and glorious Christmas mornings that are much too short.

I know now what they are trying to convey is what a child will call upon you *to be* and *do*.

I know now how a child will change your life.

Because I have a child.

M̲Y first thoughts on the subject of my child were how the child would carry the man.

I thought: this baby is my beachhead on new generations.

His arrival made me feel that all my identity, all me, mine, my and I of me had suddenly been extended into a surer, more certain future, as quietly yet with the same magnificence of a giant span being lifted into place between two shores.

I luxuriated in a special sense of well-being. His coming had not in any way given me a strange, uncertain feeling that I was being replaced, but rather a quiet, calm assurance that my replacement was here. For the time when he would be needed.

My second thoughts waited at a respectful distance until my first thoughts, and all the handshaking, cigar-passing, slap-on-the-back joviality had disappeared down the hall.

My second thoughts brought my first realization of my new role.

My second thoughts were of how the man must carry the child.

I KNEW I would have to teach a child a million little things — to balance a bike, to tie his shoelaces, that the capital of Ohio is Columbus. I guess I assumed that having a child would involve no more than these little lessons, and lots of love.

I know differently now. I know that when you teach a child to divide five into ten, the lesson has a beginning and an end. But when you teach a girl to become a woman, or a boy to become a man, the lesson is as long as your life.

And to forget to teach, or to be too tired to teach, or to elect not to teach doesn't do away with the job. It simply changes the lesson, for nothing teaches indifference or apathy more clearly or quickly than indifference and apathy.

As a man I have also been allowed to do my thinking casually and incompletely, and if I chose, to come to no conclusions at all.

As a teacher, I must spend much less time in that small, cozy hideout in my head where thoughts are strewn carelessly about, waiting for me to make them into convictions or crumple them up for their lack of logic.

Now that I am his teacher, my child will see to it that I no longer just think of my thoughts, but that I *say* them. And if I don't he will wrench them from me with his questions. And he will watch to see how consistently, and how courageously, I handle their consequences.

IF I teach any children of mine nothing else, I want them to know and understand the absolute, profound and positive relationship between happiness and love.

But I plan to give them no long lectures on love. In the first place, I know of no way to tell them *why* I love their mother. And how much I love her is not something I can say, but something they must see.

I will not even try to tell them that they must search for a love that looks and sounds and seems as great and as good as ours. I think only that I must show them that loves like ours exist.

Day by day I think you can give children some reassurance about love. I think you can show them that a love that is made well to begin with is very much like a silver chalice that's made well to begin with; I think you can teach them that the years don't, in any way, diminish its capacity; that time cannot tarnish it beyond what a gentle touch can wipe away in a moment; and that a single flower brought to it for no real reason on a rainy day can brighten it almost beyond belief.

It seems to me that I must tell my children that the happiness of human beings is too often measured or referred to in unrealistic lengths of time — in happy *years,* or a happy *life.* I want them to realize that life is not lived in lifetimes or even seasons, but in sunny mornings and snowy afternoons, in picnics in the yard and on Tuesdays with the flu and in hours and minutes and in waiting for a child's fever to break and sitting quietly with your husband or wife on a Wednesday night or picking up her dress or his suit at the cleaner's. That if they can't find happiness here they won't find it next week or next month somewhere over the horizon, in the excitement of flying an airplane or climbing a mountain or accepting the honors of their fellow men or of kissing a strange new mouth.

I am going to tell any child of mine what I believe — that the clearest indication of a happy life are happy days and happy nights, that the clock, and not the calendar, will always tell her truthfully whether happiness is really hers.

When I was nine years old I bought a squirt gun at Kistner's Drug Store with a quarter that rightfully belonged to the Lincoln School Lawn Fete. Until I finally confessed the fact to my mother, I spent three of the longest and most dreadful days of my life.

I think a parent owes a child a good grasp on the subjects of honesty and integrity. I believe they are difficult virtues to understand and apply, and a young man or woman dealing as they someday will with money, ambition, and ego in the world of making a living, will no doubt face a few troublesome trials.

I will spare a child the Pilgrim Placard of the Past, "Honesty is the Best Policy", for that will be no more helpful to him than a bookful of algebra answers when he doesn't understand the path of logic leading up to them. Nor do I want him to hear from some inept do-gooder that not taking an apple or a dollar bill that isn't his in any way proves honesty, for in truth, it indicates little more than the value of the objects was below his level of temptation.

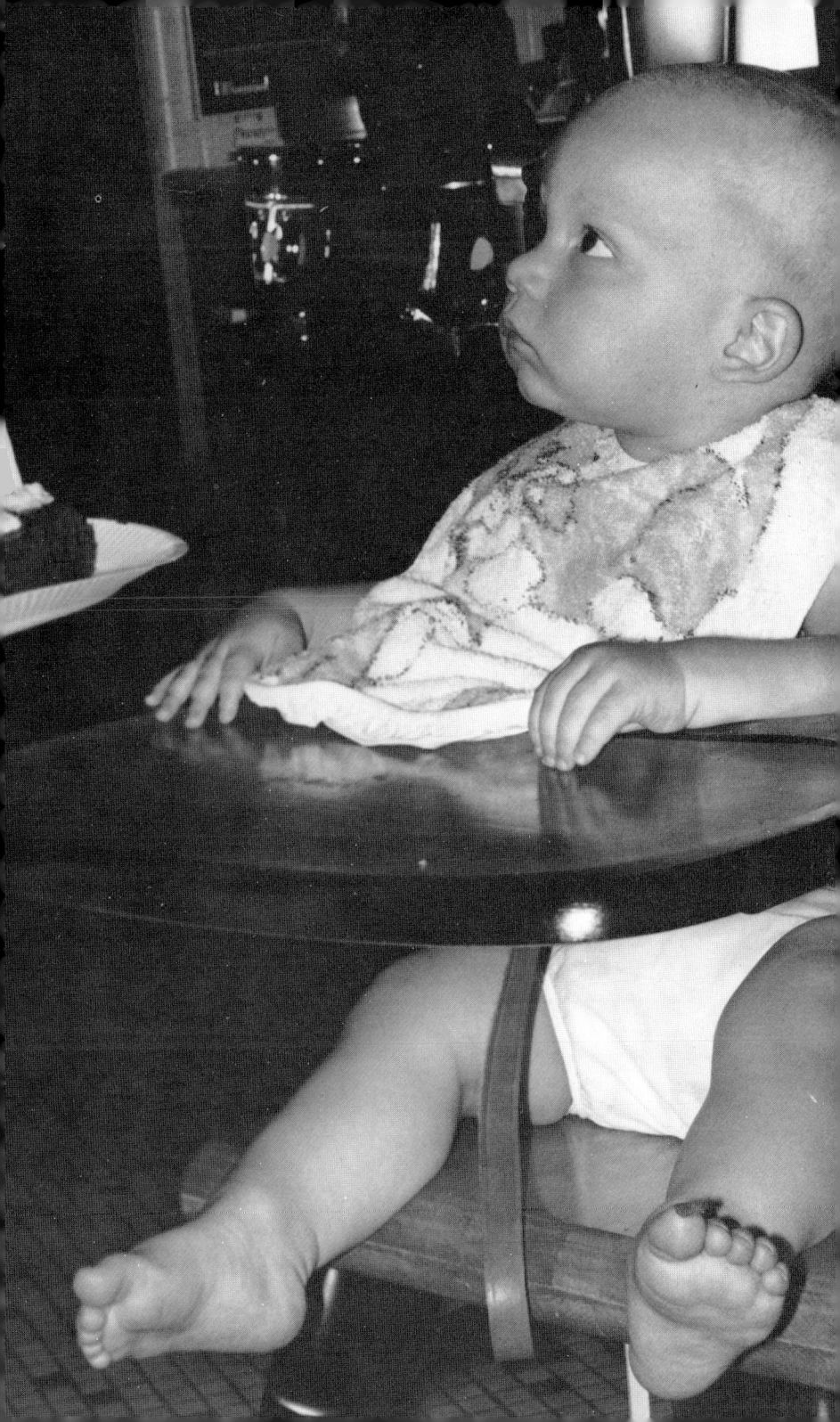

I want him to know that small acts of honesty may only be pride or pomposity or fear or deviousness in disguise.

And when my girl or boy is old enough, I think I can make her understand something about the consistency of true honesty — of integrity — by telling them the story about the woman who said she would sleep with a man for twenty thousand dollars but was so infuriated when asked if she would sleep with him for five dollars that she cried out in anger, "What do you think I am?" To which the interrogator replied: "We have already established that, Madam. What we are trying now to determine is the price."

I want any child of mine to know as much about honesty and integrity as I do, which is that they seem to be good companions that help us like ourselves and live more comfortably with the critical consciences most of us have. Honesty and integrity seem to be good friends that attract others to us, perhaps because we seem to perform consistently and therefore our moves and motives appear trustable.

Honesty seems to be a good, though sometimes uncomfortable, guide to follow in our decisions, personal and professional, so that we seem to know who we are, what we are, and what to do next. And integrity seems to be closely related, in its effects at least, to its engineering counterpart, "integrity of design". That is, human integrity seems to have the same advantages of structural integrity — both seem able to hold things together through hell and high water.

If I tell a child no less or more about honesty and integrity than that, he'll know as much as I do, and he can weigh it all on his own scale.

I may be able to tip that scale slightly if I tell him the squirt gun story at just the right age. Especially if I tell him the whole story — that the squirt gun can probably still be found in the rafters of the garage where I threw it; that I never had the heart to fill it, even once, with water.

Most of us start our children off in life by telling them there is a Santa Claus, an Easter Bunny, and a God.

When the child seriously begins to doubt the Easter Bunny, we tell him we were just kidding about that. When logic and the little boy he walks to school with won't let up on the Santa Claus question, we smile and blast his North Pole dream into oblivion. But somehow we hope he'll go along believing in the only one of the three he's never even seen a picture of, and the only one who makes difficult demands — to forego the fun of teasing the dog and the joy of punching Joey Selkirk, all with no promise of tangible reward.

I don't think I'm going to ask my girl or boy to believe more than they can about God. I think if you try to paint God too vividly in the mind of a child you only confuse him and create irrelevent questions about whether He wears a hat or not.

I think a child of mine will have a better understanding about God if I reverse the order in which religion is usually taught. Rather than begin with God and work down to people, I'm going to start with people and go the other way.

For I believe if there is a God, He wants us to understand first that the world is about people, that we'll get from them no more than we give, that we will always be happier human beings when we love than when we hate, when we help than when we hurt. Then, knowing that, if my son or daughter someday decides that God is simply an old world word for Good, nothing really changes, except perhaps at the very end.

One thing sure, I will never allow anyone to teach them to *fear* God, for it must be confusing to a child to hear God identified as a Good Guy on one hand, and then be told that He also is watching from behind the garage with the power to strike him dead if he displeases Him.

If my child accepts God as a friend, then I think He's got to be a good friend. Someone who can be trusted twenty-four hours a day to be kind and patient and understanding to a little girl or boy. And if someday I give my youngster two dimes and tell her one is for her and the other for Sunday School, and if she inadvertently drops one of them in the lake, it won't bother me a bit if she feels secure enough in the relationship to react by saying, "Oh, oh, God. There goes your dime."

I WANT a child of mine to know that, though he will find that the world is full of tricks, there is only one bit of real magic in this life that can truly move mountains and turn dreams into things he can touch and feel and see and enjoy.

And that magic is called "Believing in Yourself".

I want him to know that almost everyone can achieve whatever he *thinks* he can achieve, that great doctors are great doctors, great carpenters are great carpenters, great pilots are great pilots, and great failures are great failures because they believed exactly that much in themselves. That bad breaks or big brains are rarely factors.

I want my girl or boy to know that America put men on the moon not because it suddenly discovered some secret that no other nation had turned up, but because it decided it would put men on the moon, and set about learning what it had to learn and building what it had to build to get them there.

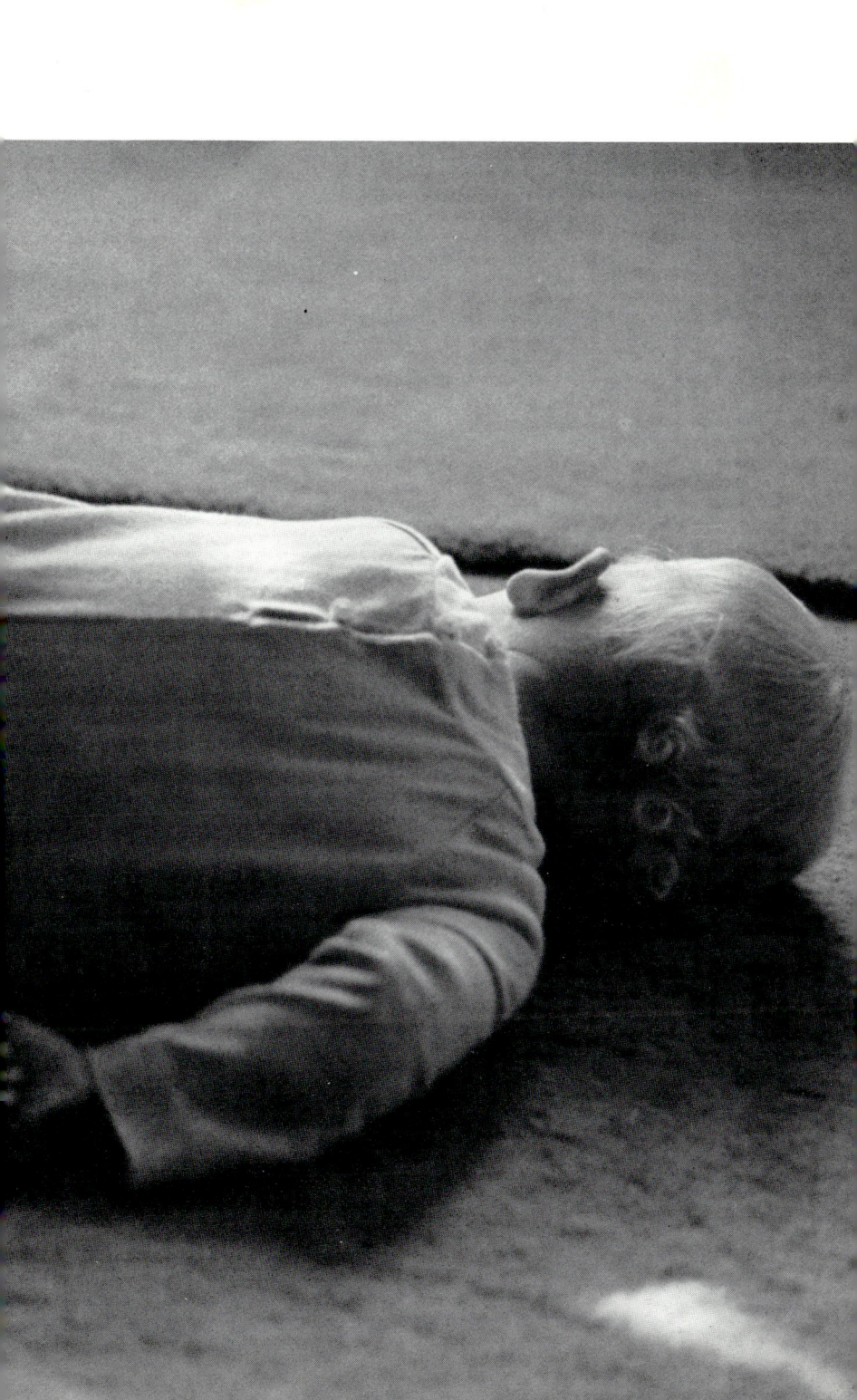

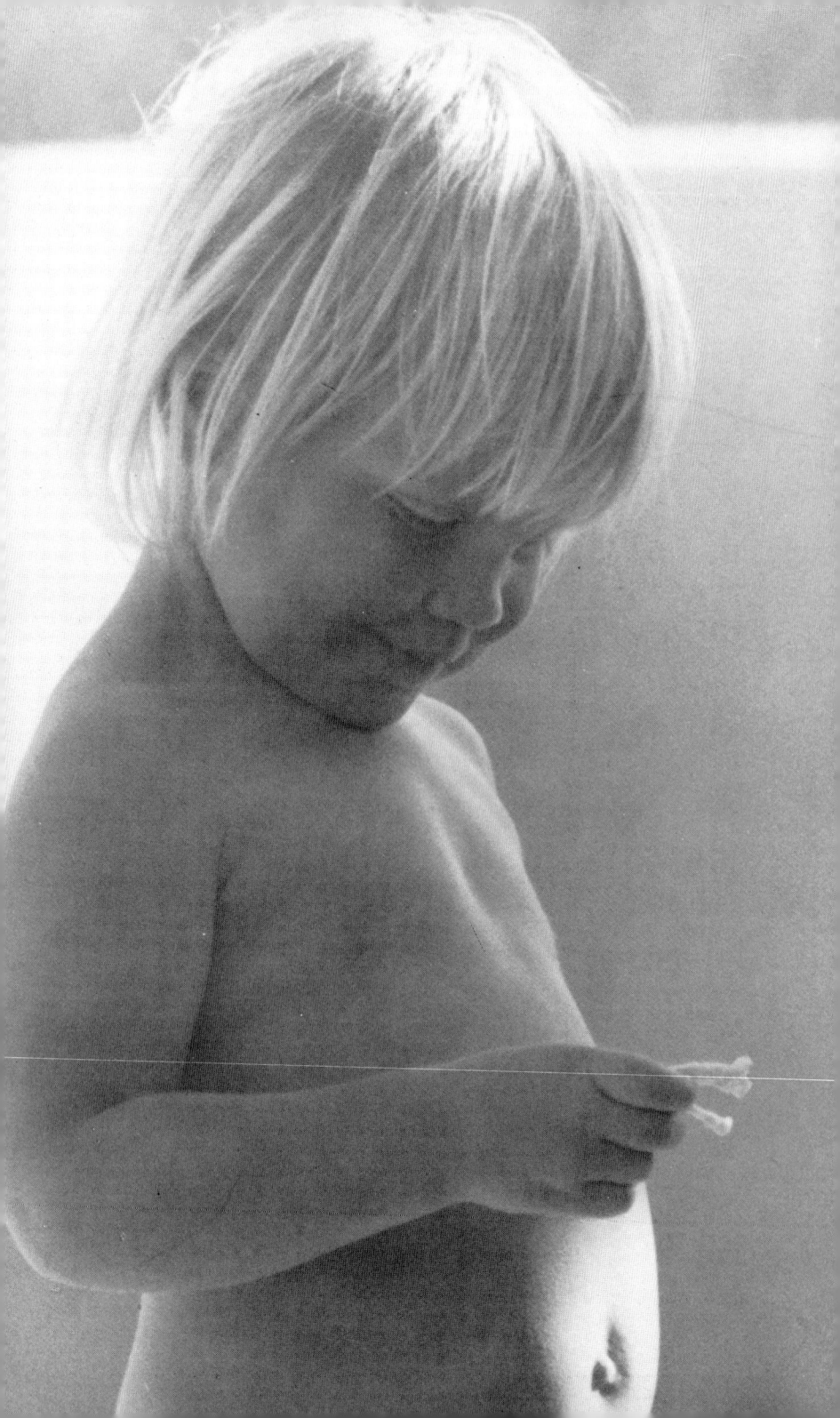

I want a child to understand that, if he believes in himself, he can use his energy to work toward what he wants to be or do, and not in wondering whether he's good enough to try. For worry will wear him out as fast as work, and worse, will tie him to the starting line.

I realize that making my children begin to believe in themselves is up to me, that it is not as simple as getting them to say it. I know it is a sensitive and subtle business that starts early and maybe never stops, that when they can't seem to throw a ball straight, there's a big difference between laughing at them or saying: "You are really throwing it far, and as soon as we straighten it out, every team in town will want you." I realize if they want to play the piano instead of becoming something or someone I have in mind for them, I must let them know I'm interested in whatever different drummer they're marching to and want to hear him, too. I know the importance in saying to a child in the middle of a family discussion, however important or unimportant, "What do *you* think?"

It seems to me I should warn a child that sometimes, whether it's eight more pages of arithmetic or eight more years of medical school that do it, frustration and fatigue may make him doubt he can climb that mountain. And that, for a little while, he may have to call on courage and run on fear. But that if he'll just hang on long enough to get to the tree line, confidence will rejoin him there and take him to the top.

I'm sure as he grows up, my child will learn a hundred magic words, from Abracadabra to Hocus Pocus, which he'll hope will heal all the rips in all the clothes he wasn't supposed to play in.

If I do nothing else, I'm going to teach him the seven best words of magic *I've* ever heard: "If you think you can, you can."

WHATEVER kinds of lives my children may want to lead, they will have a need for people — people they want to help and people they will feel a need to help. There will be people my daughter or son will want to like them, to love them, to praise them. But unless they understand that the part of a person they see is simply a shell, simply a place to hide the fears and the hopes and the prides and the prejudices and the irrationalities and the nerve endings that are lurking just below, then they will forever be confused by the inconsistencies and strange behavior of their fellow human beings.

There comes a time in the life of an infant when he begins to examine himself — his fingers and feet and toes. And because he comes to understand these parts of himself so well, he is not confused by them when he sees them in others.

I want to teach my child to do exactly the same thing with his mind and heart and soul — to examine his own — then use them as a gifted guide in his relations with others.

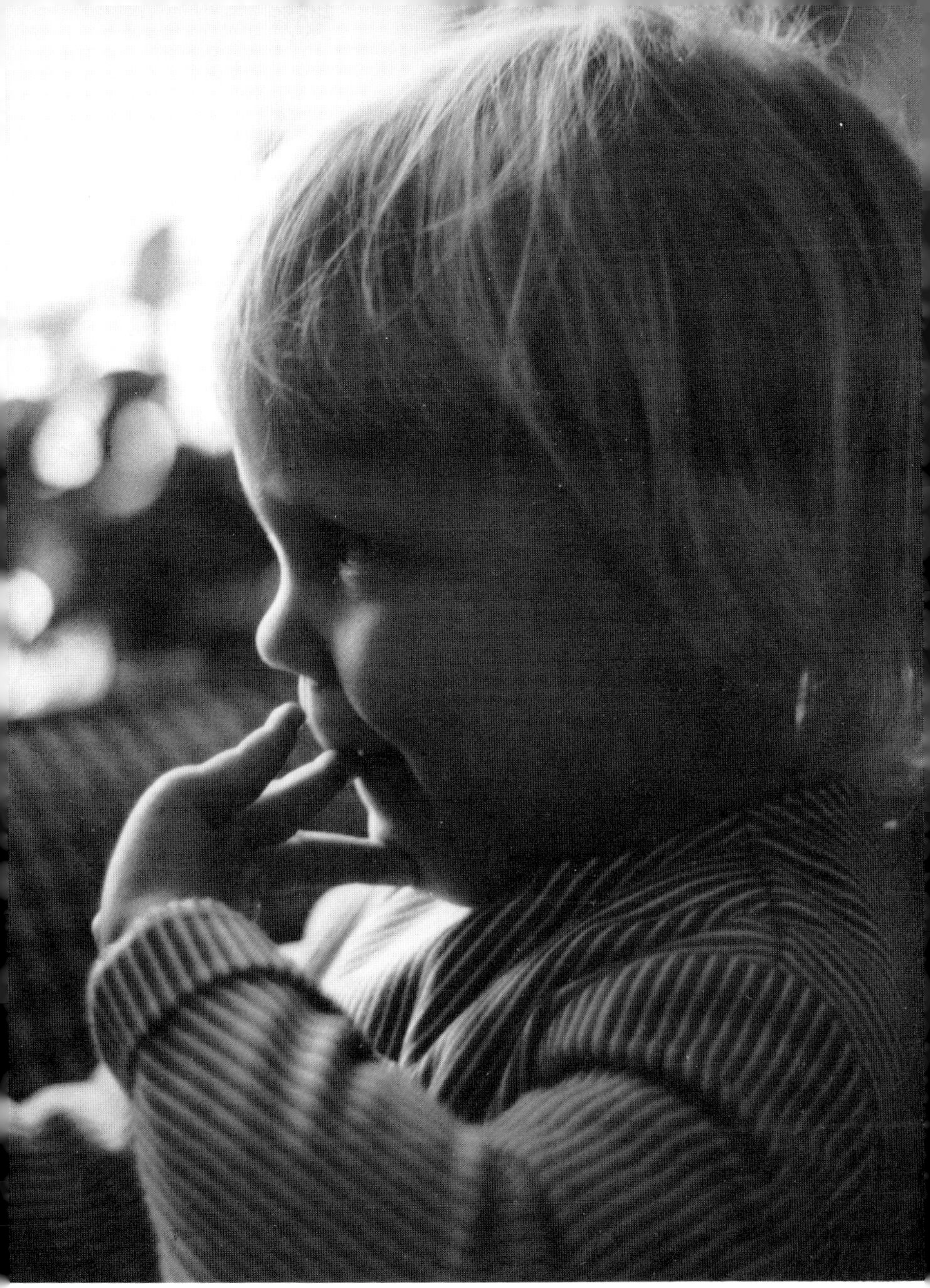

If he is sensitive enough to recognize how often he hides what he *really* feels or wants in order to keep from showing to others his greed or pain of dissapointment, then he may understand that the rest of the people in this world do exactly the same thing.

If he is honest enough to admit that he sometimes wears a Halloween Mask of serenity and self assurance to cover anger that may be raging inside, he may be wise enough to know that the outward calm or courage in others at the center of a storm may simply be fear that is saying its prayers.

I want my child to know that however sober, serious, callous, arrogant or flip a friend might appear on the surface, she will still cry quietly in the bathroom when a pimple appears at prom time, or when she feels unloved or unsure or threatened or confused.

I want my child to recognize that many people who will go to great lengths to impress him with their brilliance or cleverness or great ability will have little ability or none at all — that some of the most ordinary of us are the ones who go to such great lengths to appear to be extraordinary.

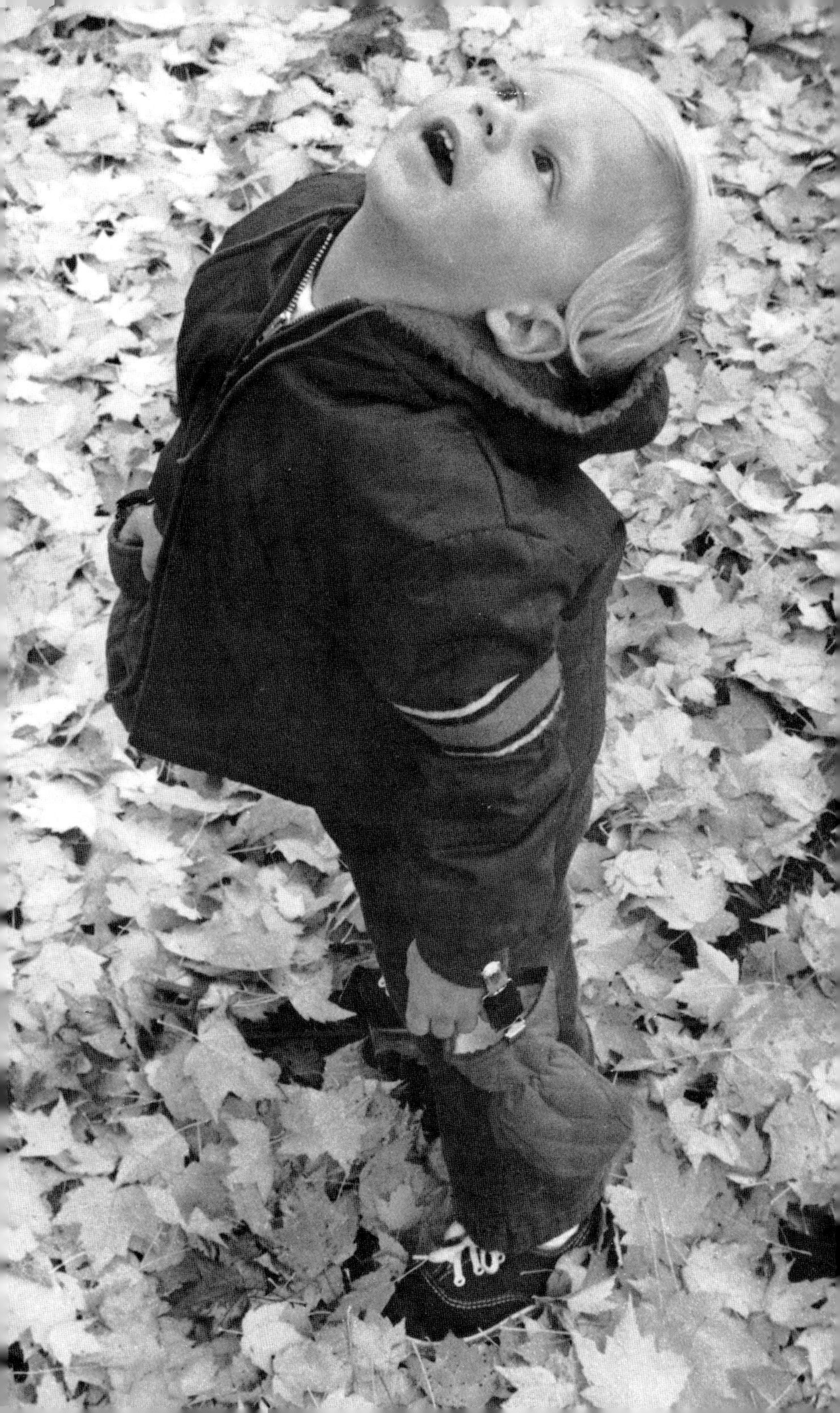

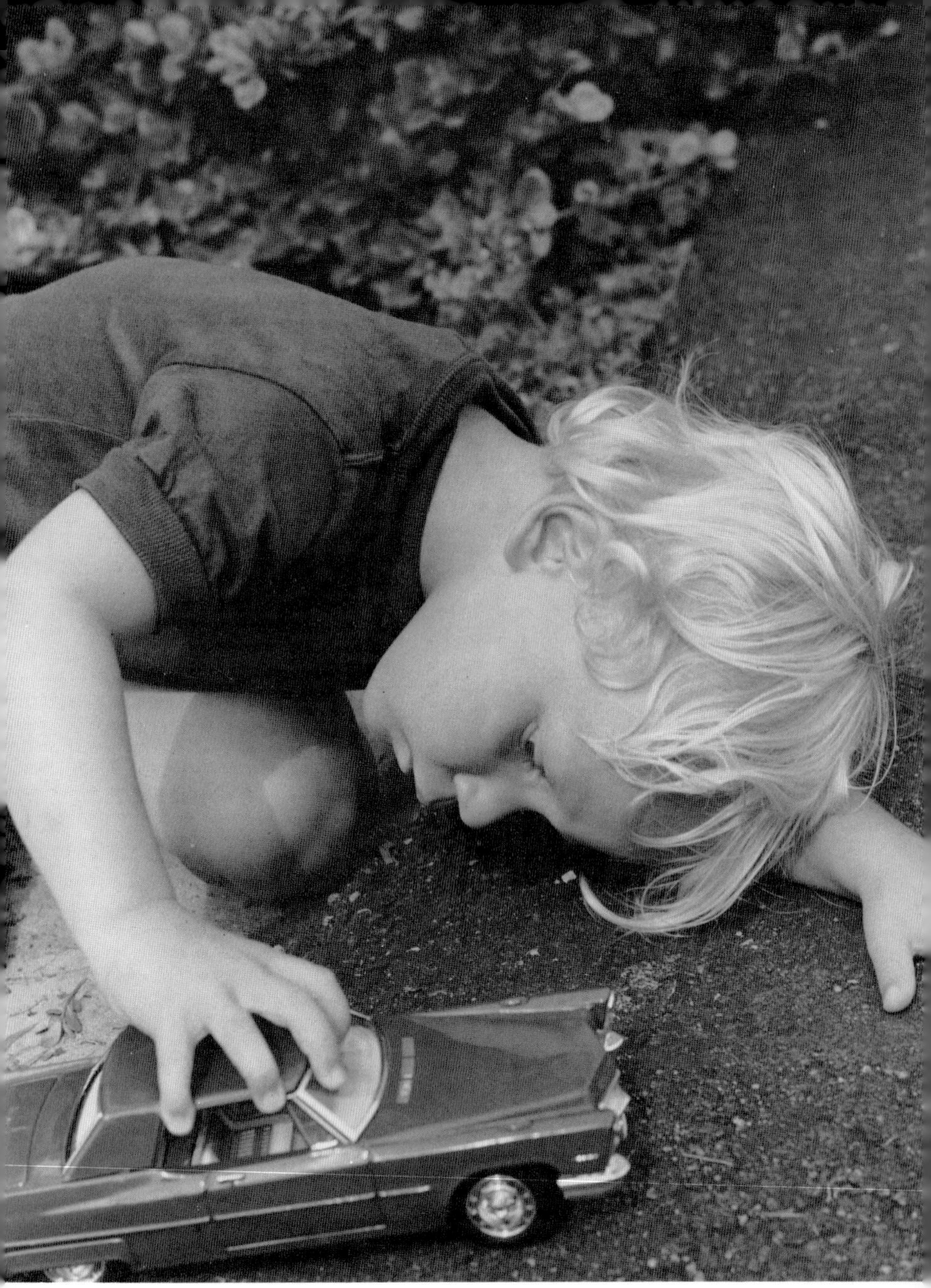

I want my boy and girl to know that each of us, no matter how much religion or psychology we have mastered, are strongly self-oriented; that in spite of the fact we may be willing to die for someone who is dear to us, we think mainly about ourselves in any given day, about *our* happiness and health and hopes. Even what we'll have for dinner tonight.

I want my child to know that each of us has a theme song that few of us will admit, but that even as we deny it we act it out in almost everything we do. It is a song of life and a song of death. It is a song of truth and of the present state of the art of humanity, like it or not: THERE WILL NEVER BE ANOTHER ME.

Knowing all these things will change none of them. But if they add to my children's understanding of people and to their ability to relate to them, they may well deepen their ability to love, broaden their capacity to forgive, and give them a little more peace of mind and happiness than their neighbors across the street.

And I'll settle for that.

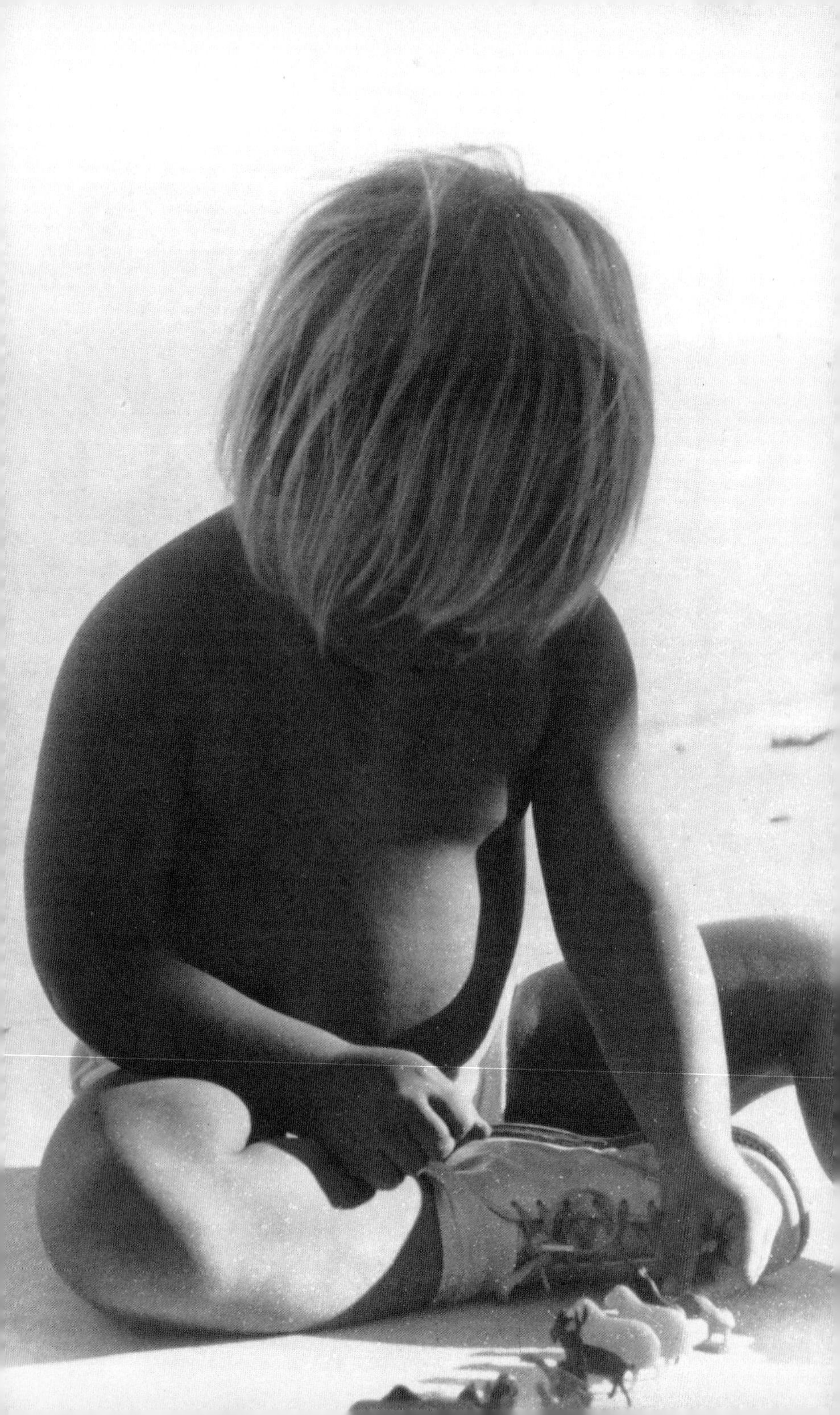

SOMETIMES my son will sit in schoolrooms for what seems to be forever, waiting, hoping, praying for the bell to ring and release him. When it does, he'll rush out with nothing more in his head than when he walked into the class. And he'll sit in other classes and hope the bell never rings, completely caught up in and mentally recording everything that's being said or shown.

Sometimes my daughter will go to doctors who will quickly examine her and prescribe a few pills that will make her feel no better than before; sometimes she'll go to doctors who will listen carefully to her symptoms, move their hands surely and silently and slowly over her body, and quickly tell her exactly what is wrong and what to do about it, and she will be as well as ever within a few days.

My children will no doubt have the same experience with plumbers, mechanics, lawyers, carpenters, with directors whose movies they see, writers whose books they read, cooks whose food they eat.

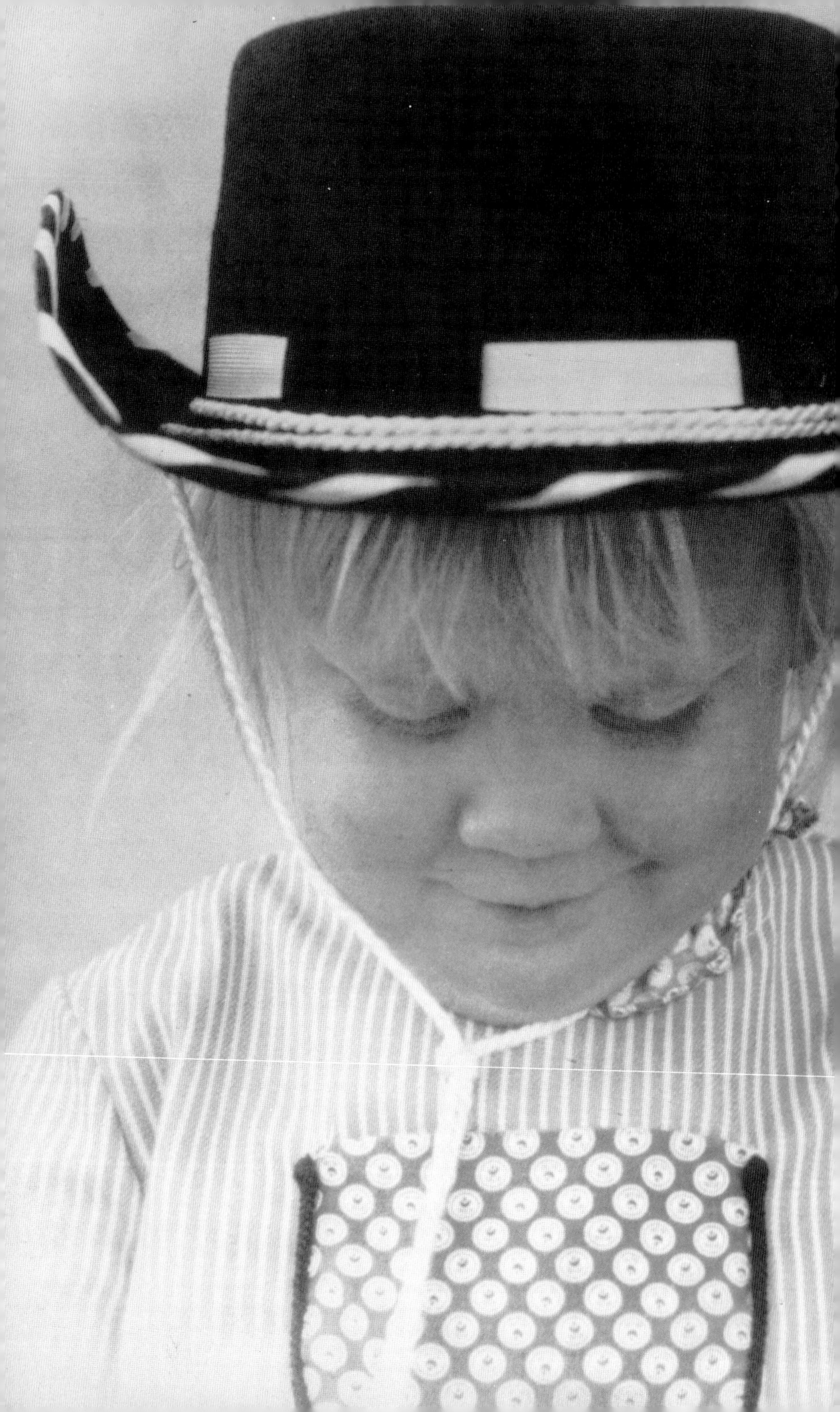

So before they have to live long enough to come to the same conclusion themselves, I want my children to know as early as they are able to comprehend it that *there is nothing like a good man or woman.* And that whatever they most want their work to bring them — money, respect, praise, security, satisfaction — becoming and being *a good man or a good woman* will bring them all to them sooner than any other honest scheme they can devise.

But I want them to know I don't agree that "anything worth doing is worth doing well" (which both my carpentry and crabgrass will prove to them). Because, it seems to me, to do just one or two things really well takes almost as much time, patience, practice, care, and concentration as most of us have to give. And it is never as easy as simply going out and buying the best tools of the trade, as many poor golfers with the world's best clubs, many inept surgeons with the finest scalpels ever honed, many poor musicians with the most expensive instruments made can attest to.

So I hope a daughter or son of mine will separate a few important things that they feel will be major interests and efforts in their lives, and learn to do them well. I can promise them that if they do, the smiles they see on the faces of people their efforts touch, and the satisfaction that they will feel, will do a great deal for their sense of worth and well-being.

Maybe, when they can understand it, I will tell them the story of the old cabinetmaker who was showing a customer how well made and beautifully finished even the backs of the drawers were in a small chest he had just made.

"Why do you take such pains with the backs of the drawers?" the customer asked. "No one will ever know."

Whereupon the old man moved his rough fingers lovingly over the top of the chest and replied in a voice so soft it was almost as though he were talking to himself:

"I will know."

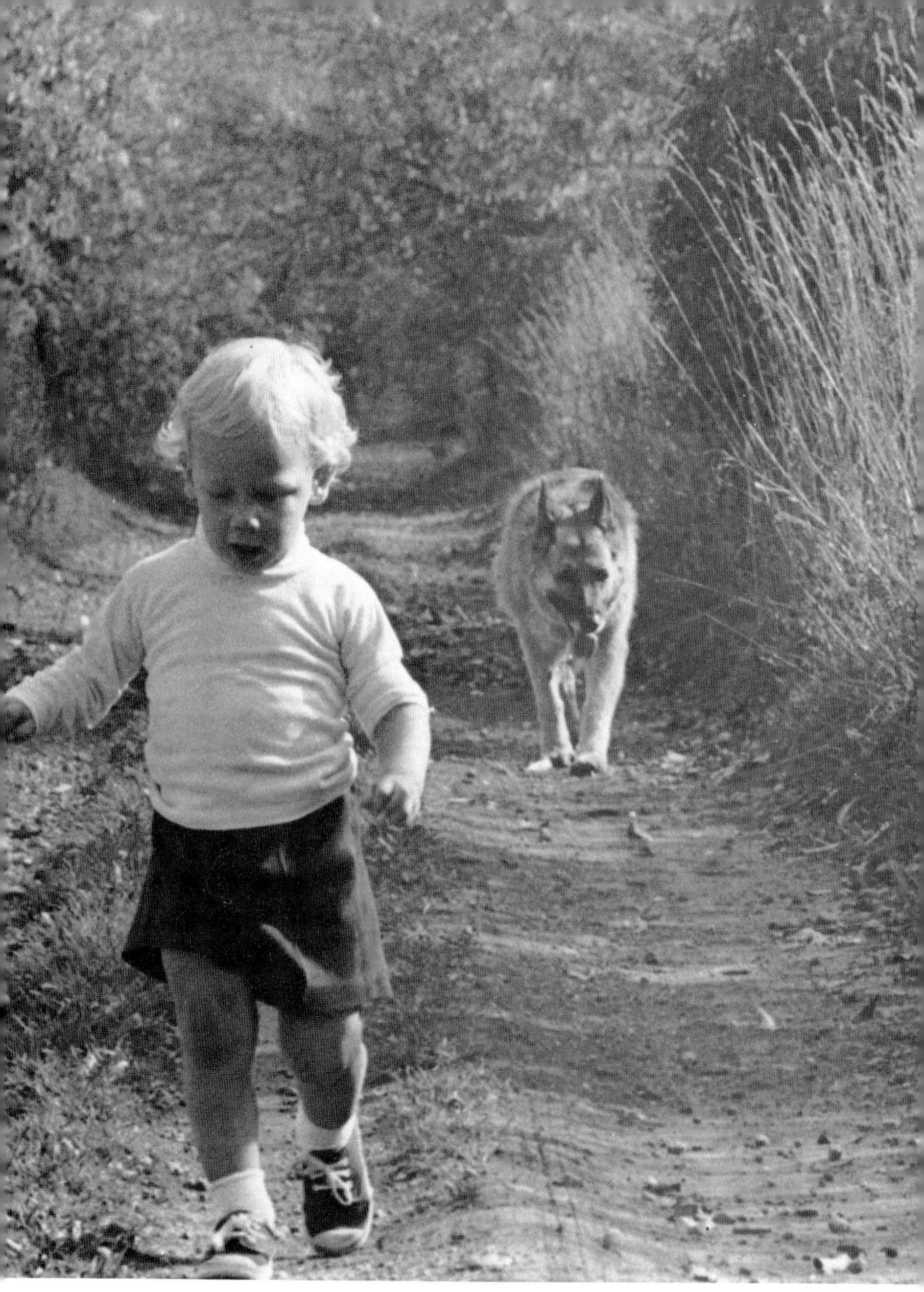

I WILL try and give a child of mine enough of a sense of security, and hope that he develops enough of a willingness and ability to *think,* that he will feel comfortable with an open mind.

For I want my girl and boy to have happy lives, which I believe will call for a constant supply of good friends of all kinds, all colors, and all ages. And I don't think, unless they learn to listen and to hold new ideas up to the light, that they can ever hope to hold onto half the good and thoughtful people they'll want to be with.

It seems to me what I must teach them is that conclusions are like cars; they need to be carefully tested and inspected at frequent intervals. And every so often, they need to be traded in for new ones. But while that may sound like easy logic to follow, my son or daughter must know that it will always seem easier and far more comfortable to let the same old wheels follow the same old ruts in the same old roads. That, on many subjects, they will always have to fight the tendency to make up their minds once and for all.

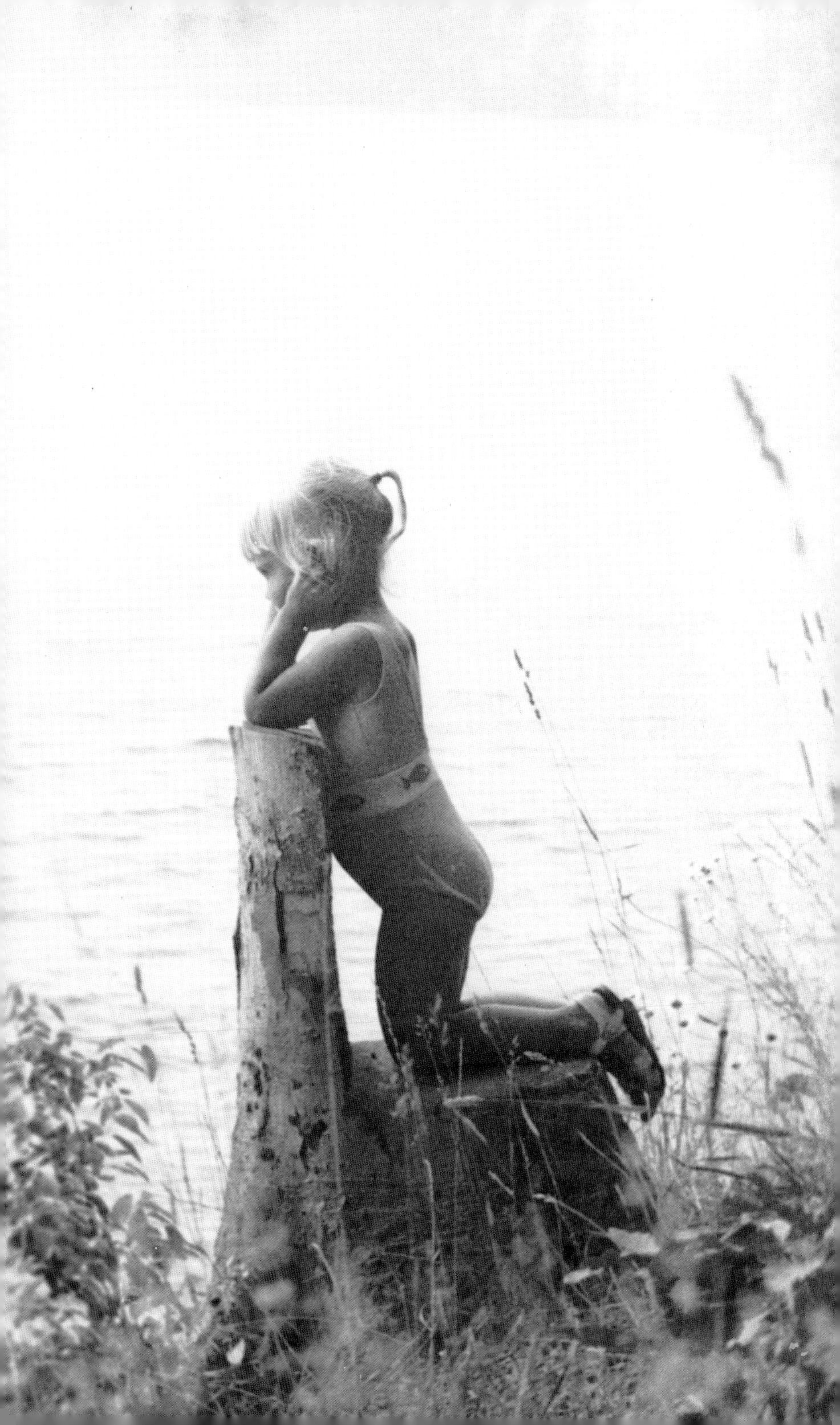

I must tell my children that they must not be afraid to question an idea even if it comes from sources they may respect — even from their mother or me. For I don't want them to confuse logic with love or loyalty, and they should know that I love and respect my father no less even though I have come to reject some of the things he believed. I love him no less because I understand *why* he believed what he did, *when* he believed what he did, which probably is to say, what logic will not let us subscribe to, love will still allow us to forgive.

I think if I teach my child to keep an open mind and have ideas of his own, that I must also teach him to preface his pronouncements with the words "in my opinion". For they will not only make his viewpoints more tolerable to others, but should serve as a healthy reminder to him that, just possibly, he might be wrong.

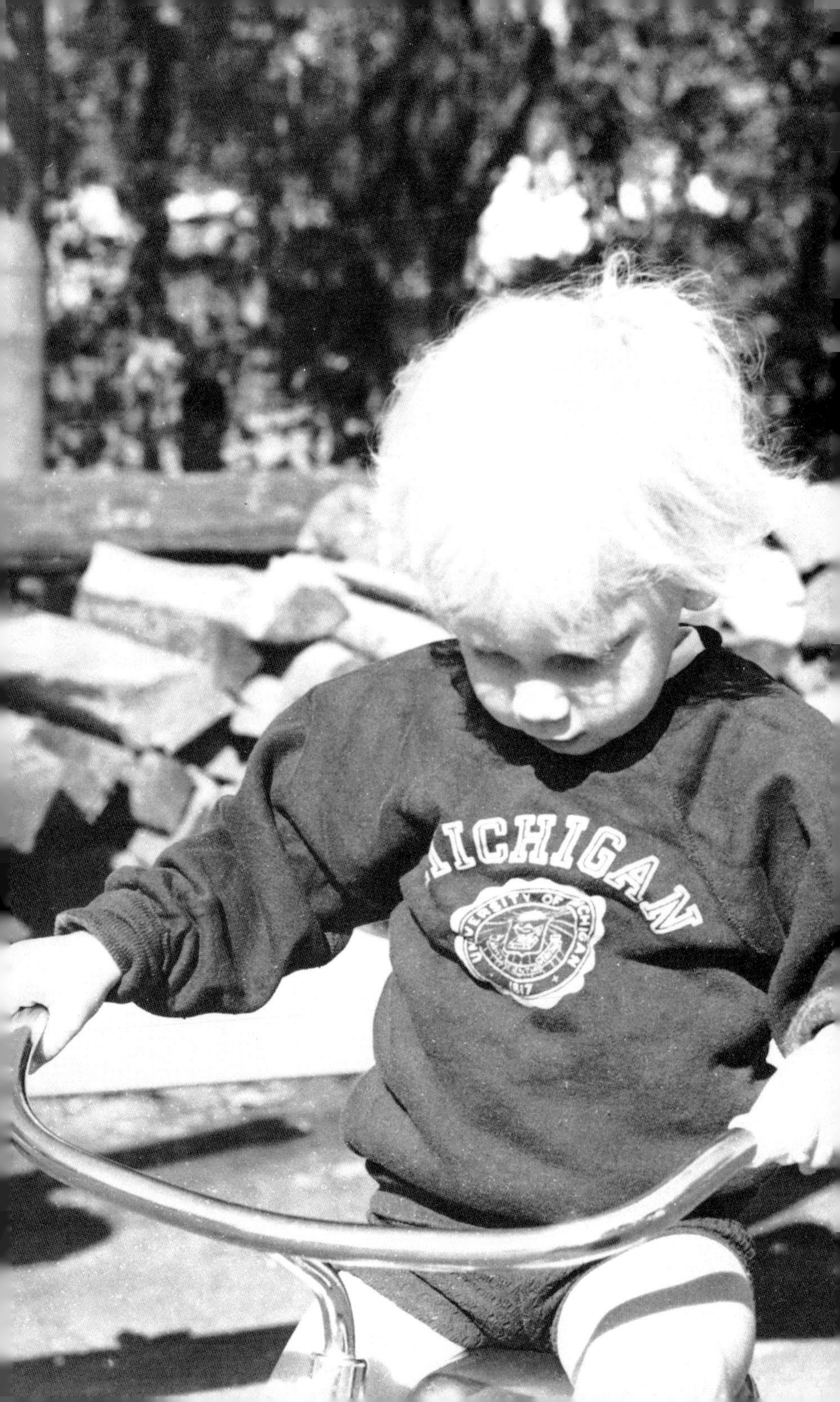
ICHIGAN
1817

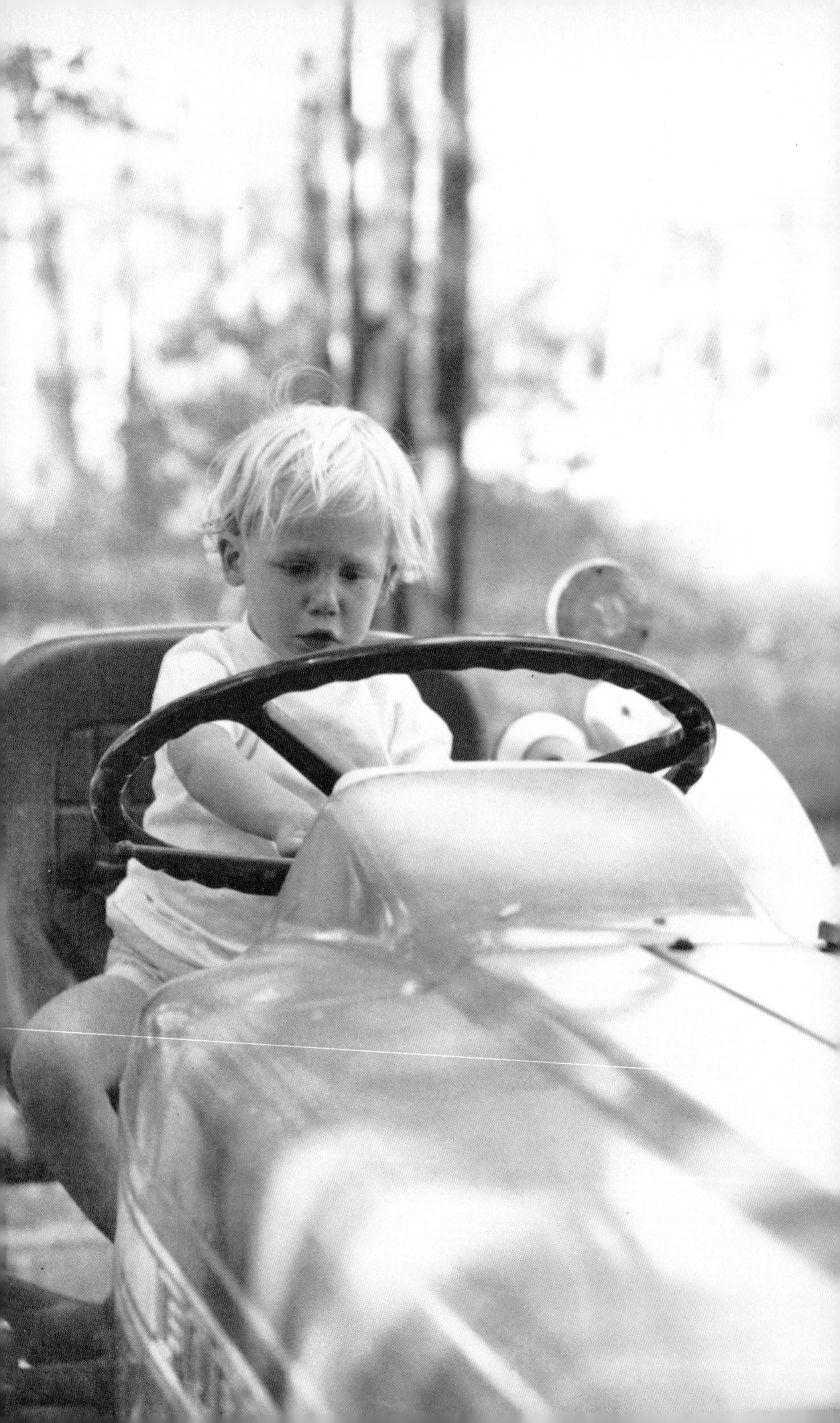

Doctors may tell my child that his health and the length of his life will depend to a great extent on what he eats. I'm going to tell him that I believe they depend even more on what he *thinks,* that the people among us with the most open minds of all — the real thinkers, the writers, the great artists and philosophers — often seem to live a very long time. I suspect that it is not because they consciously do anything about it. I would guess that because attitudes more than age or energy levels make people seem old or young, that people who never close their minds, who never mentally retire, seldom seem to let down physically or spiritually either. They are so busy rethinking their thoughts and mixing them with new ideas and changing their theories that they never seem to lose a kind of childlike appetite for what comes next, and always seem to be listening to a little voice that keeps prodding and pushing them to never miss a sunrise.

Maybe it's because they just don't believe in final conclusions of any kind.

Even their own.

*Photograph by Carol Murray.*

# AFTERWORD

Each of my four children has given me a great gift. For by making me review what I believe in and want to teach them, they have forced me to brush the dust off most of my convictions, to reevaluate some lessons that are all too easy to recite from memory alone.

My older girls, particularly, have seen to it that the dust *stays* off my convictions, and that I give life to every one of my beliefs seven days a week. For they have grown into two beautiful adult human beings, sensitive, perceptive, uncynical. Truly people who *shine*. And they watch me today harder than ever, because now we're adults together, and they want to see if I seem as right about things as we look at each other eye to eye as I may have seemed from the seat of a tricycle.

So I think the little ones and the big ones may just keep forcing me to be a better person — more understanding, more thoughtful, more hopeful, more thankful. And there could be no greater gift than that.

To give them a small gift in return, I'd like them to know about a little list of quotes I've collected and which I keep in a drawer in my desk. Some of them may mean nothing to them, and I offer them with no advice — only with the explanation that each has served me well. Some have suggested at least a starting point when I was stumped for an idea, one or two have given me courage to march into hell for what I thought at the time was a heavenly cause, some have given me hope when my head was down, some have helped me break icy silences, some have made people laugh when it was either that or cry, and some of them have even explained a reaction or two I've had and didn't understand.

I am only one; but still I am one. I cannot do everything, but still I can do something; and because I cannot do everything I will not refuse to do the something that I can do.

Some men see things as they are and say why, I dream things that never were and say why not.

When you get to the end of your rope, tie a knot in it and hang on.

When God closes a door, He often opens a window.

When you're getting run out of town, get at the head of the line and make it look like a parade.

All that is necessary for the forces of evil to take over is for enough good men to do nothing.

Mediocrity knows nothing higher than itself.

Never wrestle with a pig. You both get all muddy, and the pig likes it.

How glorious it is — and how painful — to be an exception.

Eagles don't flock — you have to find them one at a time.

Most people cannot escape the tyranny of reason.

# THOMAS D. MURRAY

Tom Murray is the Chairman of the Board of Murray and Chaney Advertising in Hudson, Ohio. His company — located in what was once a barn in the gentle rolling hills between Cleveland and Akron — creates the advertising for such diverse products as Firestone tires, White trucks, Grumman American airplanes, Brookside meats, and Smithers plant-care products.

To start an agency with his friend Austin Chaney, Tom resigned an executive vice-presidency at a large Detroit advertising agency where he was creative director of the world's largest advertiser, Chevrolet. He was also the man who created OJ for Florida Orange Juice and more nationally famous campaigns than there is room to mention here. In advertising, he is a sought-after speaker, a major contributor to leading professional magazines, and the creator of a creative test used in colleges and advertising textbooks.

But while advertising might take up more of Tom's waking hours than anything else, Tom's interests include flying, photography, and above all else, his family. Which is probably what makes him so good at advertising. "The world is not about advertising," he says, "the world is about people."

Tom Murray is, like all of us, a complicated person. In many ways, he's old-fashioned but highly contemporary; usually thoughtful yet often delightfully impulsive. A patient teacher of the young and at the same time impatient with complacency and intolerance. In other words, Tom Murray is human.

The best way to get to know a man is by what he believes in, and the best way to get to know Tom Murray is by reading this book.

It amplifies as it simplifies.

*(This might be a place to put a photo or two of the child or children that changed your life.)*

*(This might be a place to put a photo or two of the child or children that changed your life.)*